EASY PIANO

SHAWN MENDES
EASY PIANO COLLECTION

2   Call My Friends

6   If I Can't Have You

12 In My Blood

17 Life of the Party

22 Lost in Japan

26 Mercy

38 Monster

33 Never Be Alone

44 Señorita

50 Something Big

56 Stitches

76 There's Nothing Holdin' Me Back

64 Treat You Better

70 Wonder

ISBN 978-1-70513-225-8

Visit Hal Leonard Online at
www.halleonard.com

Contact us:
Hal Leonard
7777 West Bluemound Road
Milwaukee, WI 53213
Email: info@halleonard.com

In Europe, contact:
Hal Leonard Europe Limited
42 Wigmore Street
Marylebone, London, W1U 2RN
Email: info@halleonardeurope.com

In Australia, contact:
Hal Leonard Australia Pty. Ltd.
4 Lentara Court
Cheltenham, Victoria, 3192 Australia
Email: info@halleonard.com.au

CALL MY FRIENDS

Words and Music by SHAWN MENDES,
THOMAS HULL, SCOTT HARRIS,
NATE MERCEREAU and JOHN HENRY RYAN

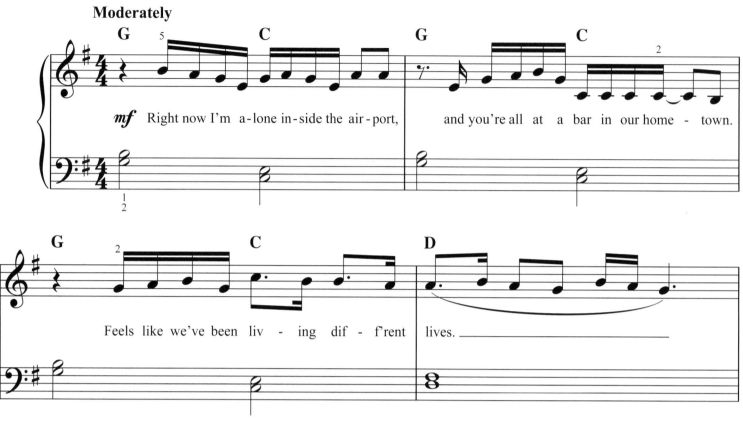

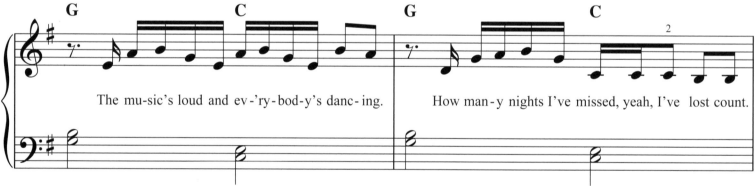

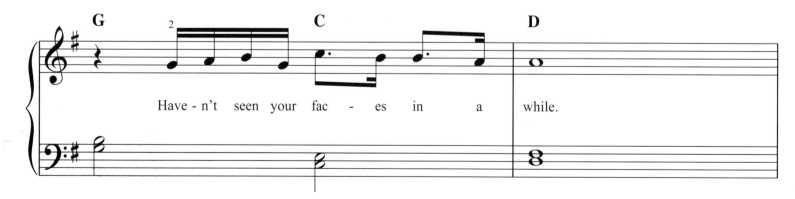

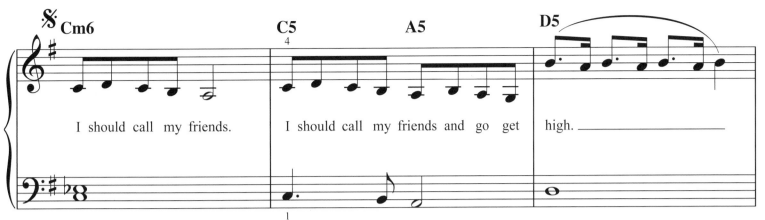

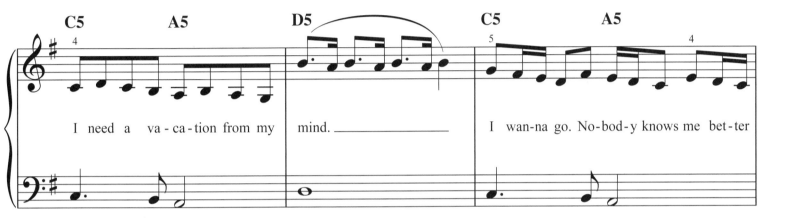

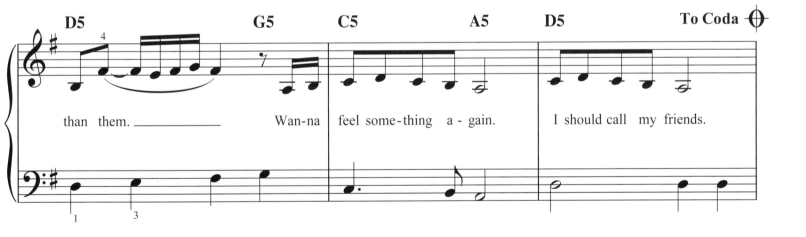

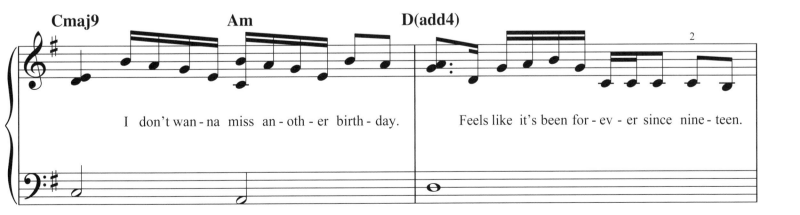

4

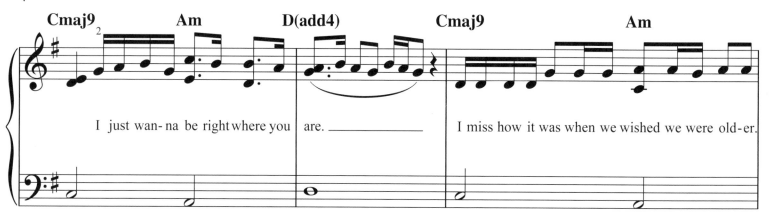

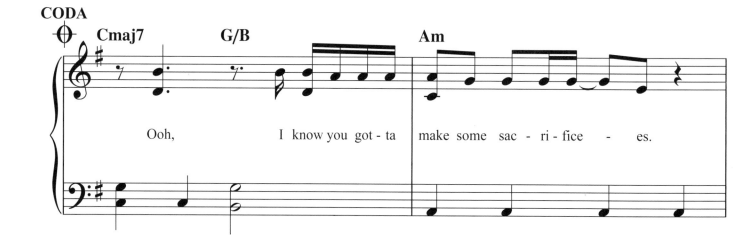

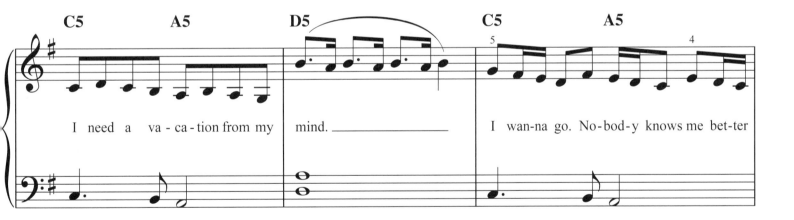

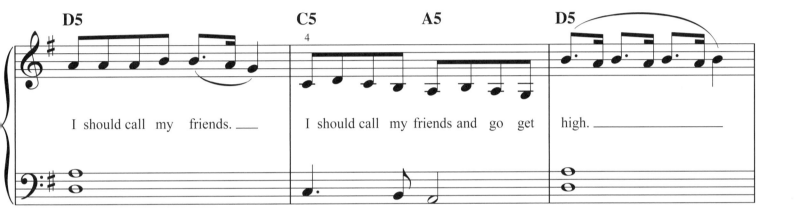

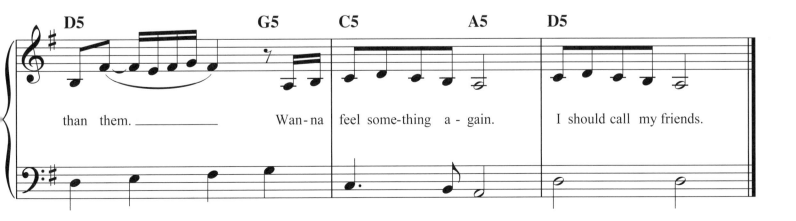

IF I CAN'T HAVE YOU

Words and Music by SHAWN MENDES,
TEDDY GEIGER, NATE MERCEREAU
and SCOTT HARRIS

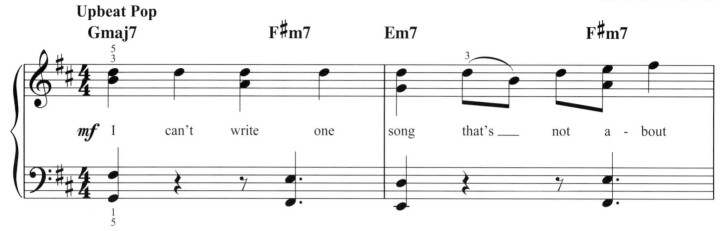

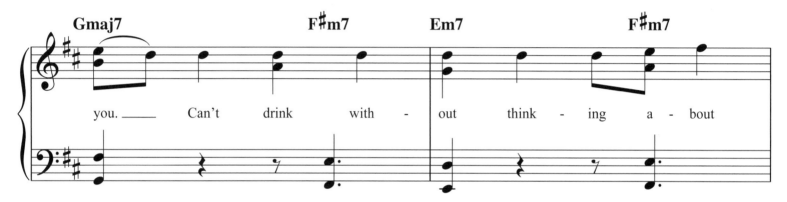

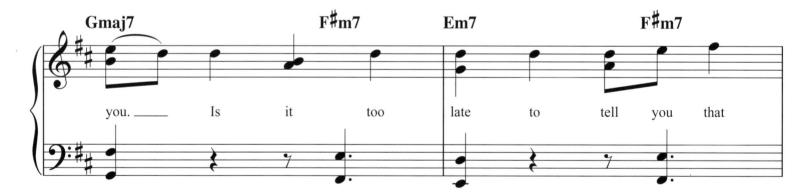

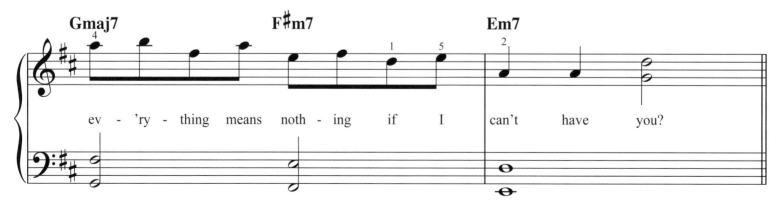

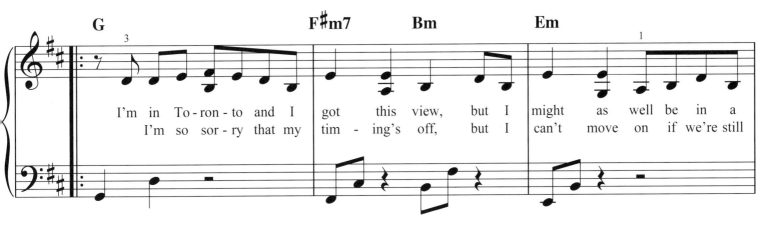

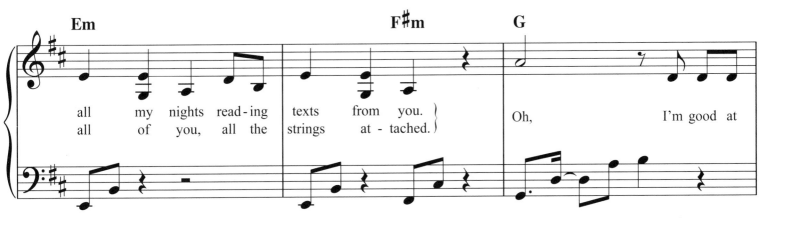

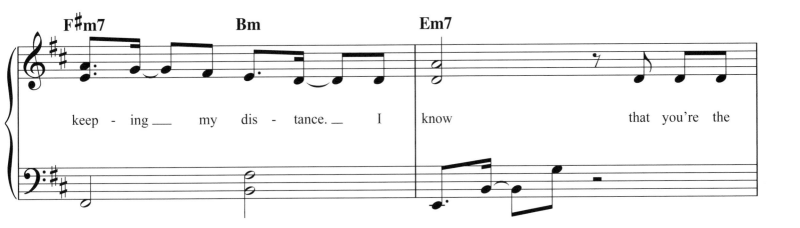

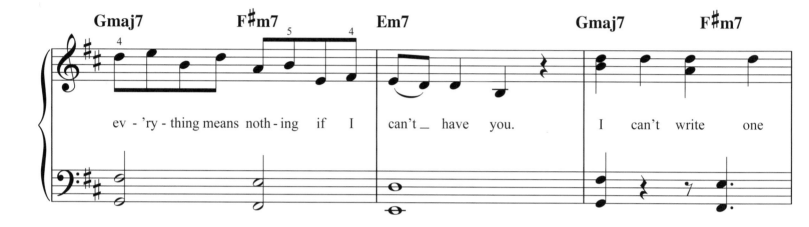

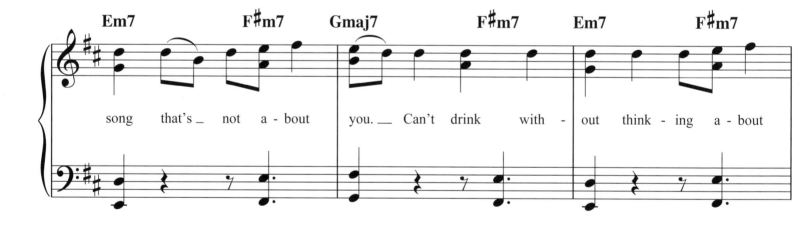

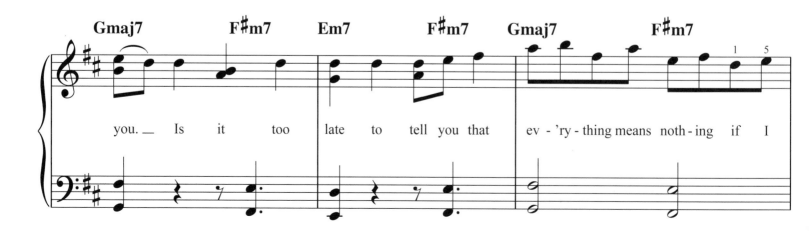

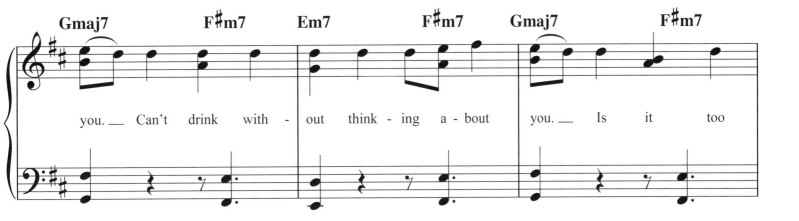

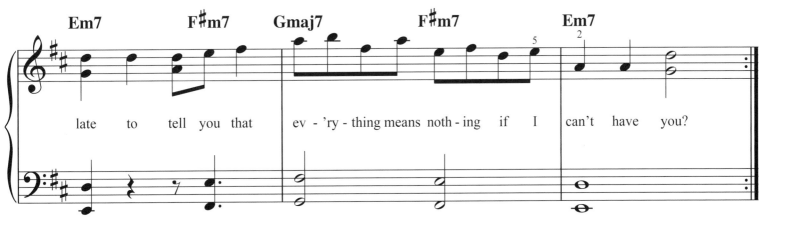

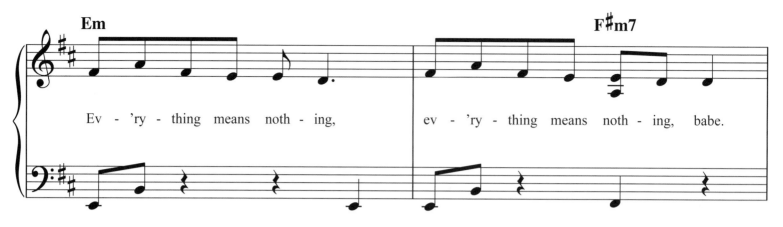

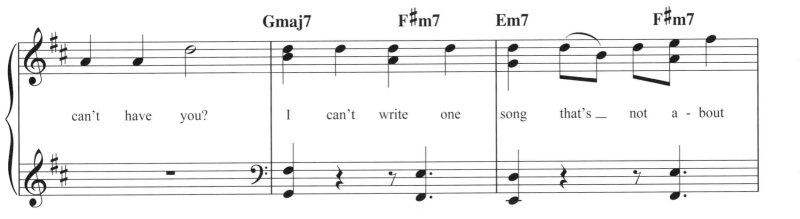

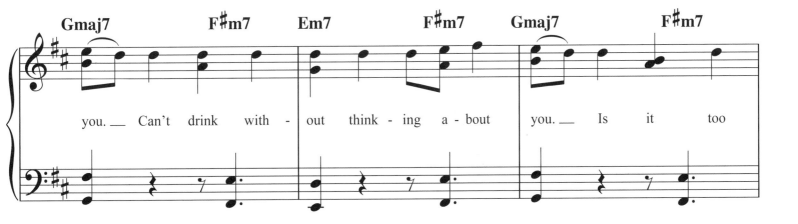

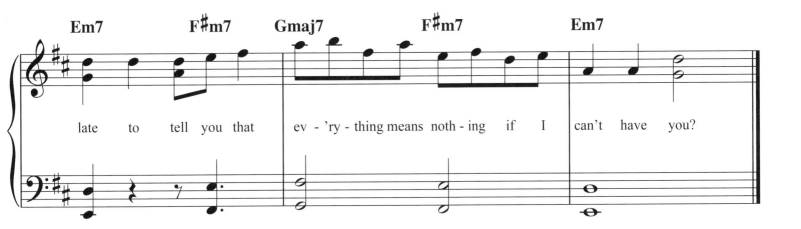

IN MY BLOOD

Words and Music by SHAWN MENDES,
GEOFF WARBURTON, TEDDY GEIGER
and SCOTT HARRIS

Slow, steady beat

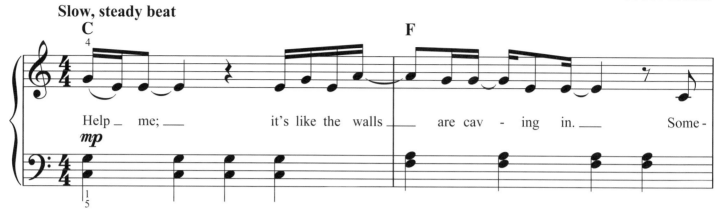

Help _ me; ___ it's like the walls _ are cav - ing in. ___ Some-

times I feel like giv - ing up, but I just can't; it is - n't in my

blood. Lay-ing on the bath-room floor, feel-ing noth-ing. I'm o-ver-whelmed and in-se-cure; give me some-thing

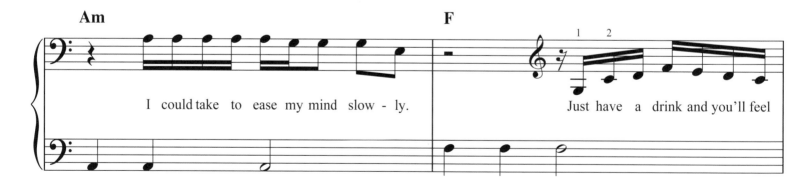

I could take to ease my mind slow - ly. Just have a drink and you'll feel

C ... **F**

bet - ter. _____ Just take her home and you'll feel bet - ter. _____ Keep tell - ing me that it gets

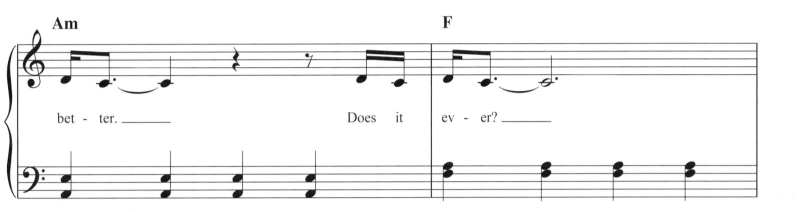

Am ... **F**

bet - ter. _____ Does it ev - er? _____

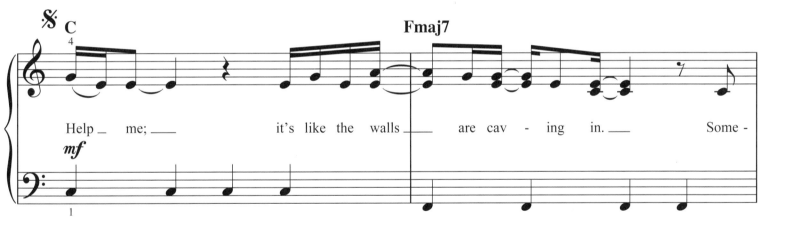

C ... **Fmaj7**

Help _ me; _____ it's like the walls _____ are cav - ing in. _____ Some -

mf

Am ... **Fmaj7**

times I feel like giv - ing up; no med - i - cine is strong e - nough. Some - one help _

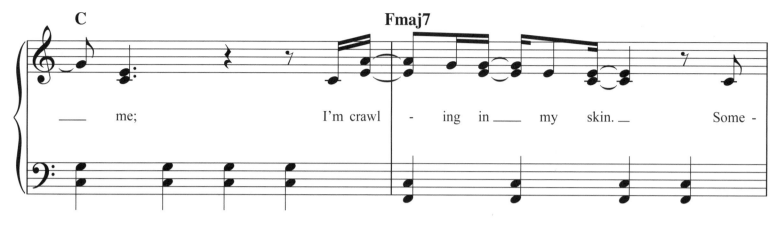

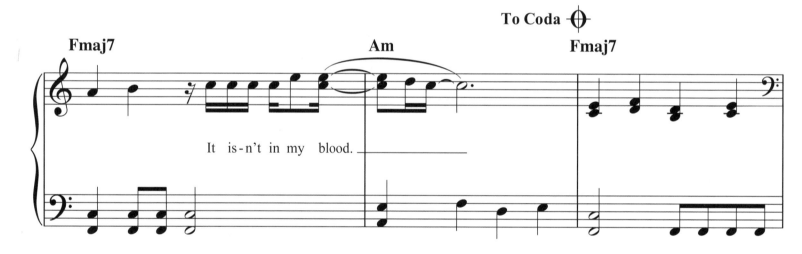

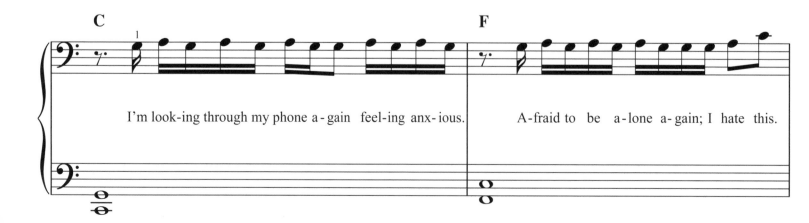

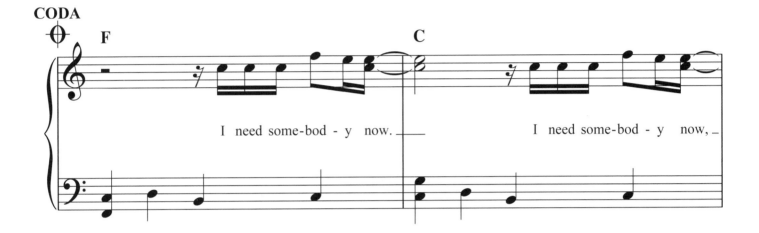

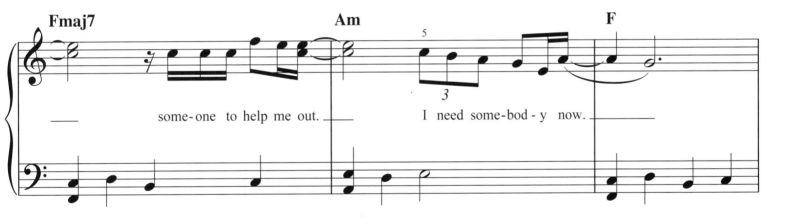

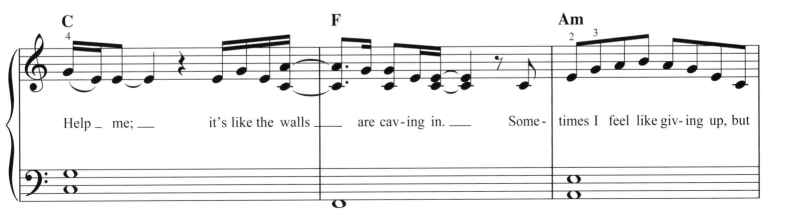

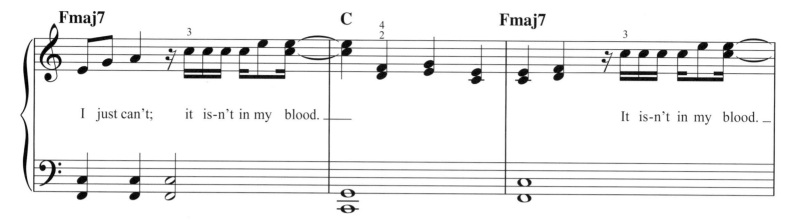

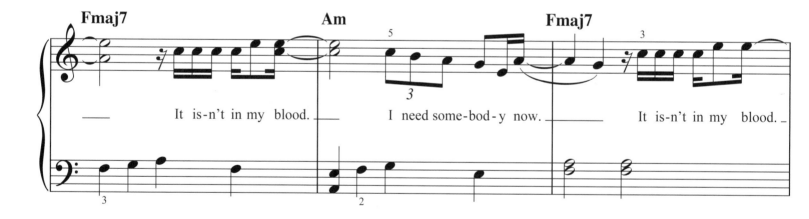

LIFE OF THE PARTY

Words and Music by SCOTT FRIEDMAN
and IDO ZMISHLANY

Half-time Ballad

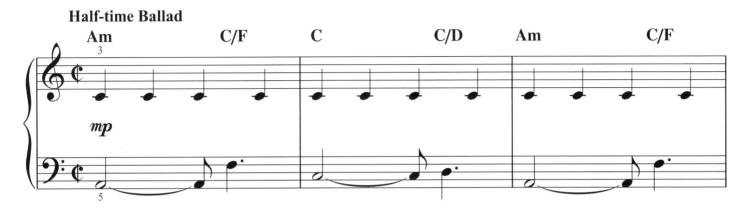

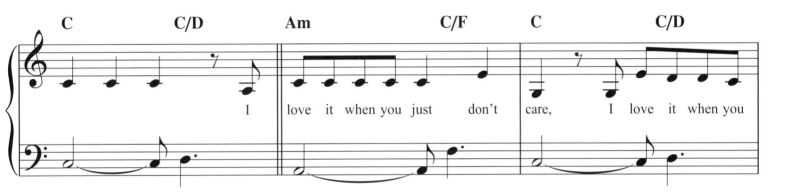

I love it when you just don't care, I love it when you

dance like there's no-bod-y there. So when it gets ___ hard, don't be a-

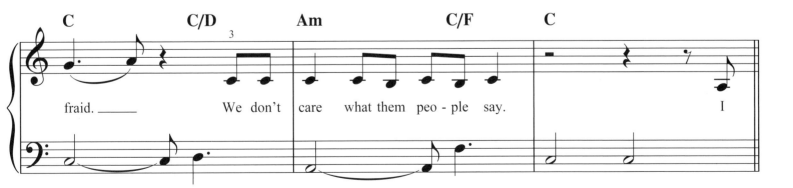

fraid. ___ We don't care what them peo-ple say. I

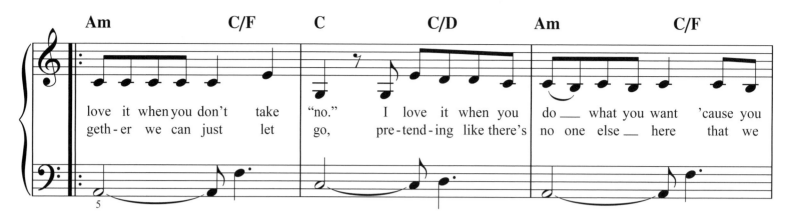

love it when you don't take "no." I love it when you do ___ what you want 'cause you

geth-er we can just let go, pre-tend-ing like there's no one else ___ here that we

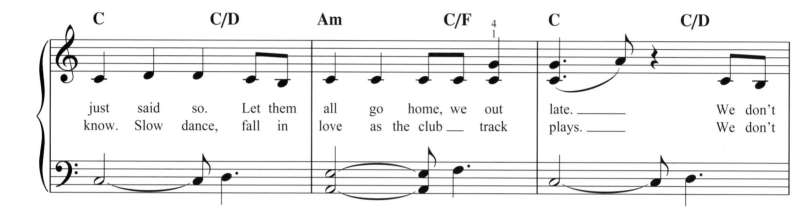

just said so. Let them all go home, we out late. ___ We don't

know. Slow dance, fall in love as the club ___ track plays. ___ We don't

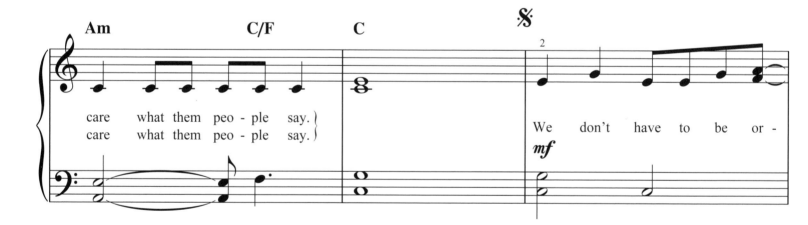

care what them peo-ple say.

care what them peo-ple say.

We don't have to be or-

mf

- di - na - ry, make your ___ best mis - takes. ___ 'Cause

we don't have the time to be sor - ry, so, ba - by, be the life of the par -

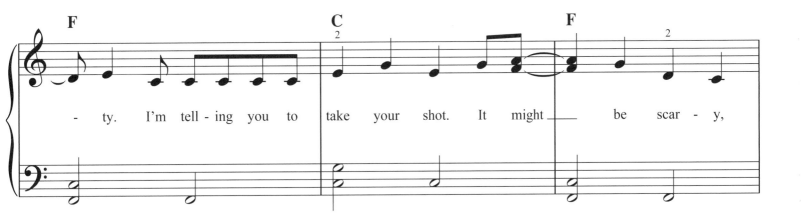

- ty. I'm tell - ing you to take your shot. It might___ be scar - y,

hearts are gon - na break.___ 'Cause we don't have the time to be sor -

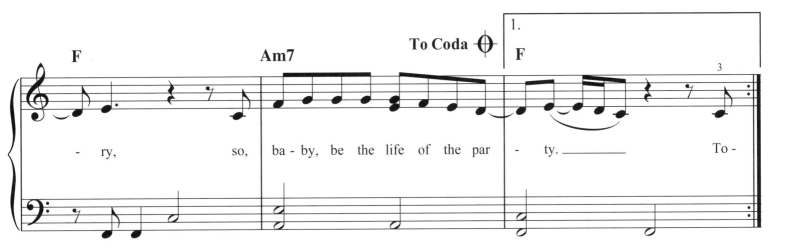

- ry, so, ba - by, be the life of the par - ty. ___ To-

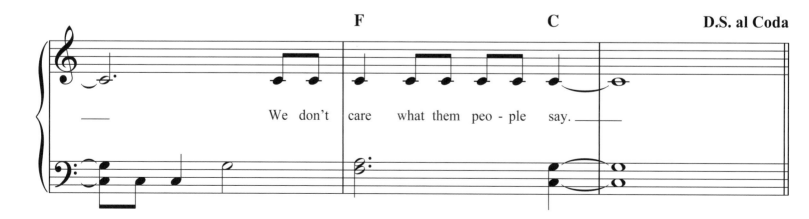

CODA

-ty. Yeah, _____ yeah, _____ yeah.

The life of __ the par - ty. _____ So don't let 'em keep you down.__

_____ Oh, __ you know you can't give up.__ 'Cause

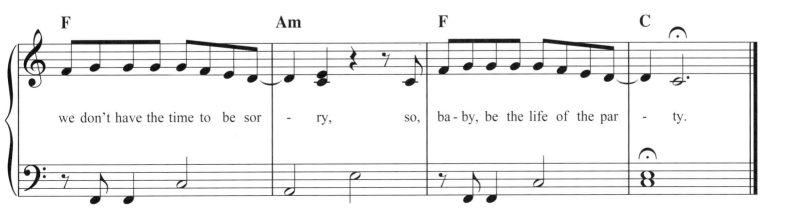

we don't have the time to be sor - ry, so, ba - by, be the life of the par - ty.

LOST IN JAPAN

Words and Music by SHAWN MENDES,
TEDDY GEIGER, NATE MERCEREAU
and SCOTT HARRIS

Freely

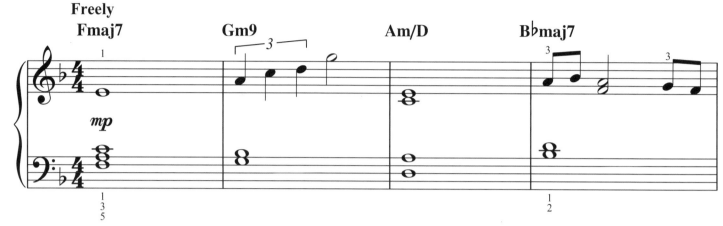

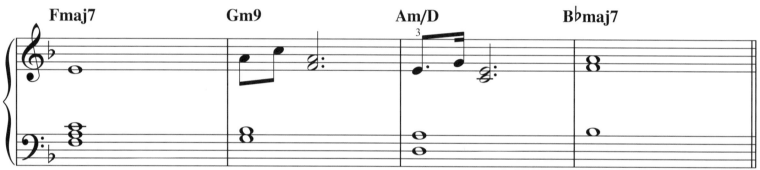

R&B groove

All it'd take is one flight,   we'd be in the same time zone.   Look-ing through your time-line,

see-ing all the rain-bows, I, _____ I got an i-dea, _ and I know that it sounds cra - zy.

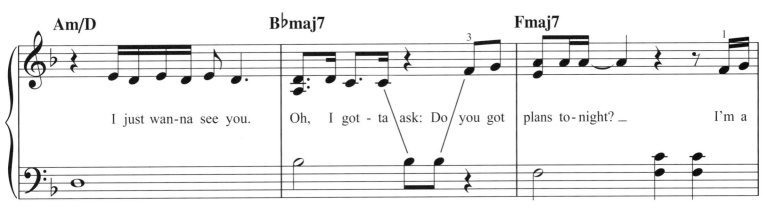

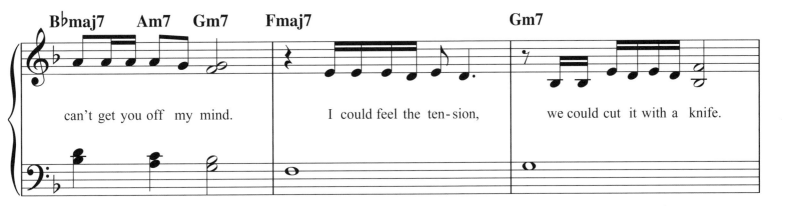

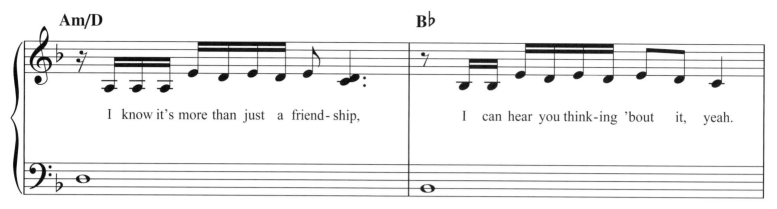

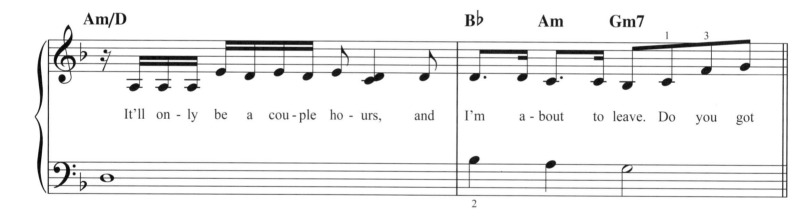

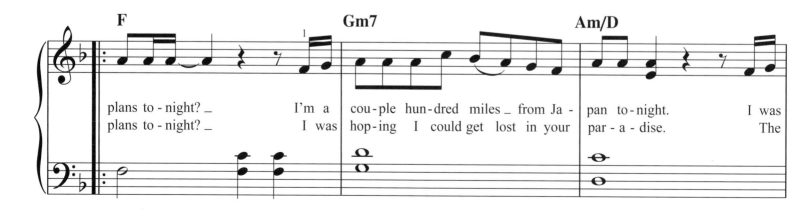

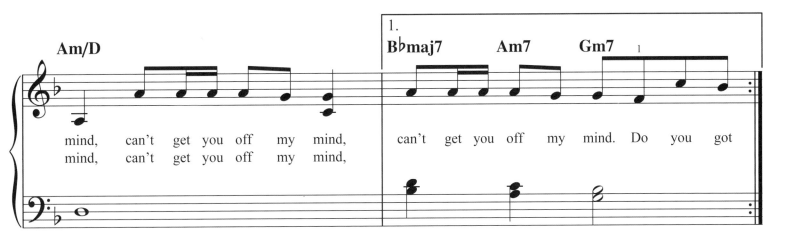

MERCY

Words and Music by SHAWN MENDES,
TEDDY GEIGER, DANNY PARKER
and ILSEY JUBER

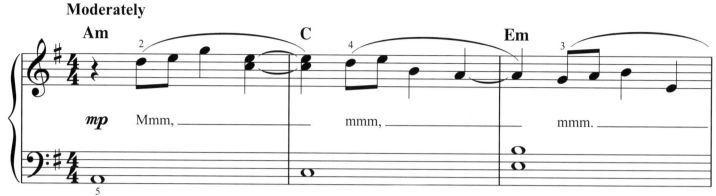

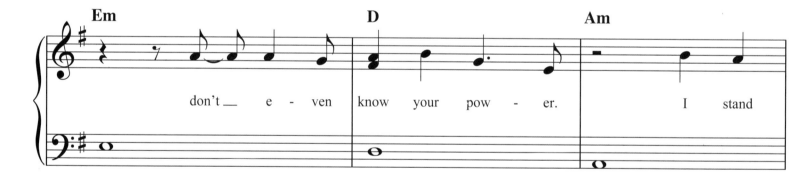

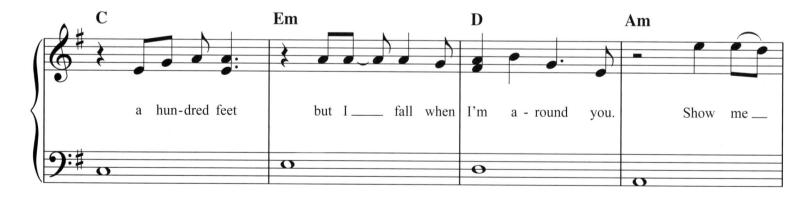

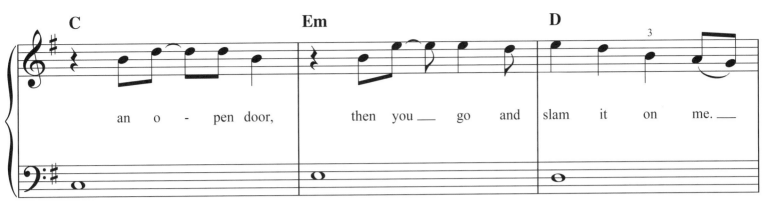

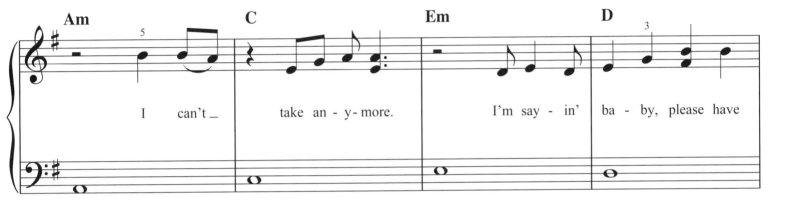

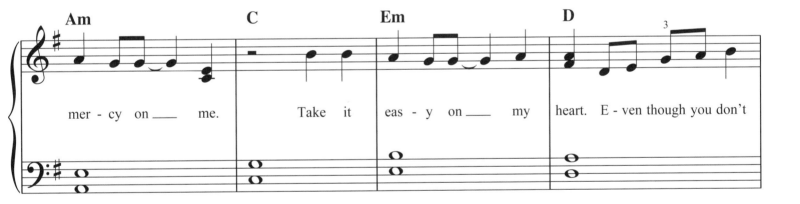

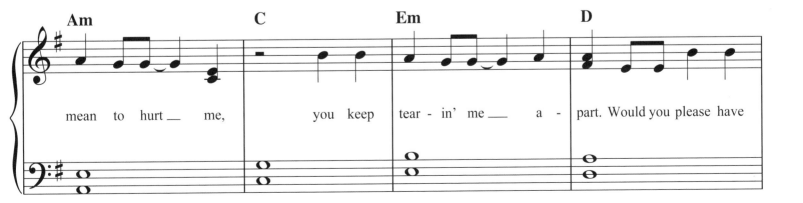

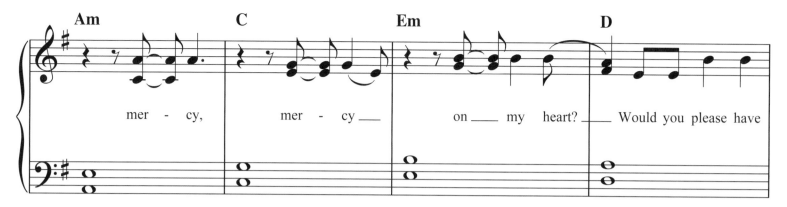

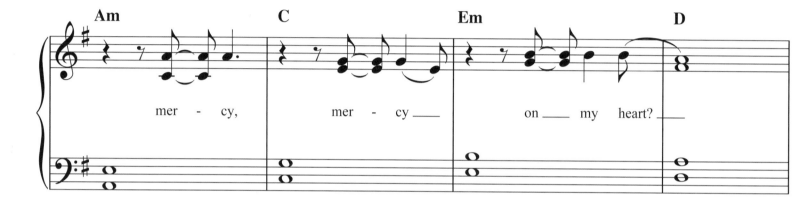

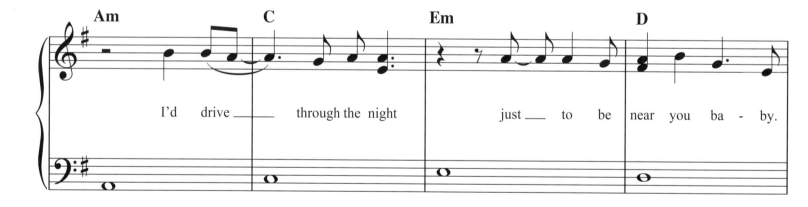

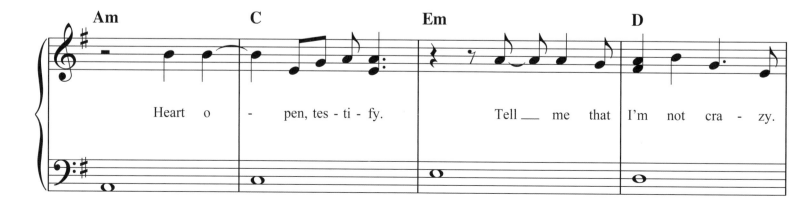

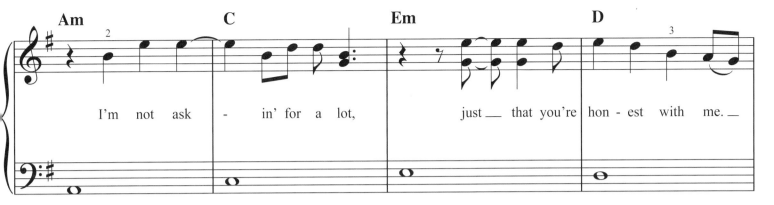

I'm not ask - in' for a lot, just — that you're hon - est with me. —

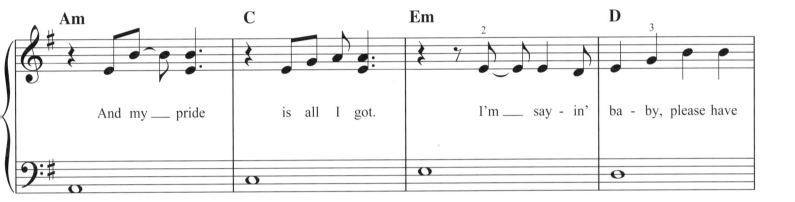

And my — pride is all I got. I'm — say - in' ba - by, please have

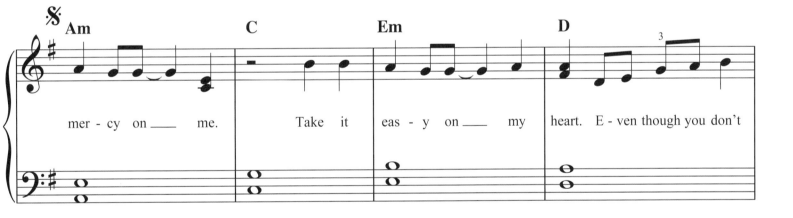

mer - cy on — me. Take it eas - y on — my heart. E - ven though you don't

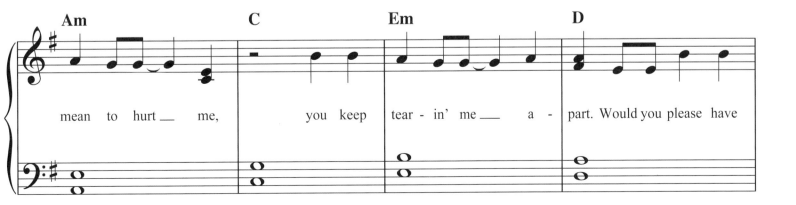

mean to hurt — me, you keep tear - in' me — a - part. Would you please have

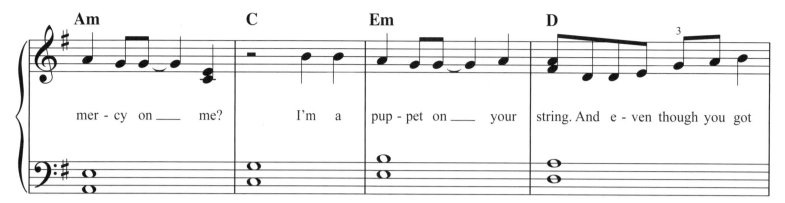

Am   **C**   **Em**   **D**

mer - cy on ___ me?   I'm a   pup - pet on ___ your   string. And e - ven though you got

To Coda

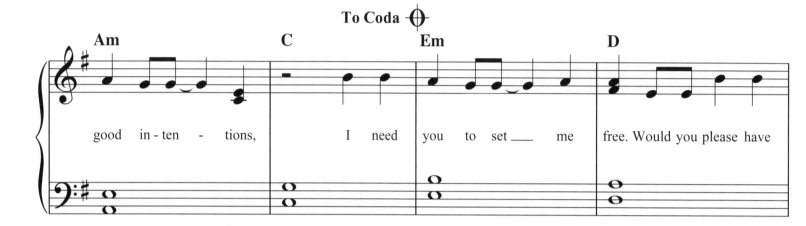

Am   **C**   **Em**   **D**

good in - ten - tions,   I need   you to set ___ me   free. Would you please have

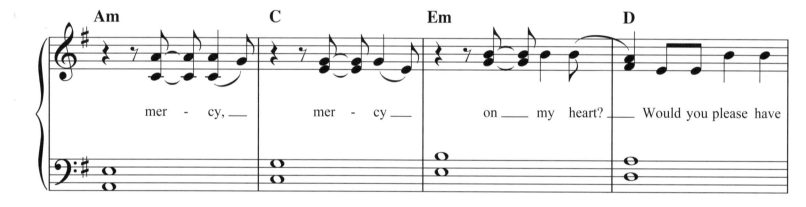

Am   **C**   **Em**   **D**

mer - cy, ___   mer - cy ___   on ___ my heart? ___   Would you please have

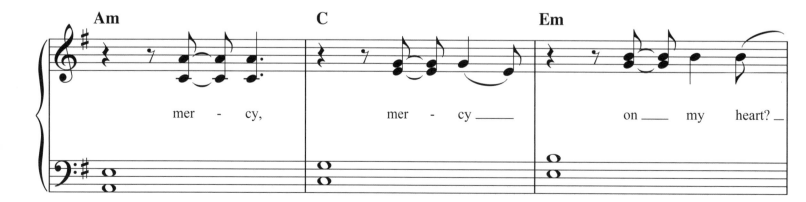

Am   **C**   **Em**

mer - cy,   mer - cy ___   on ___ my heart? __

Con - sum - in' all ____ the air in - side my lungs.

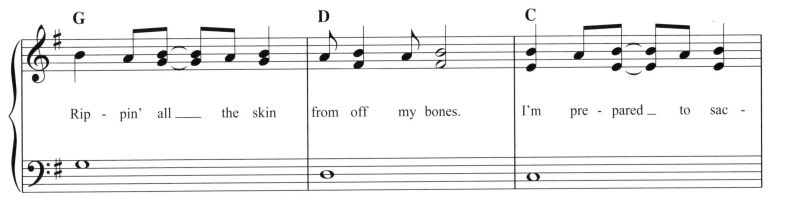

Rip - pin' all ____ the skin from off my bones. I'm pre - pared ____ to sac -

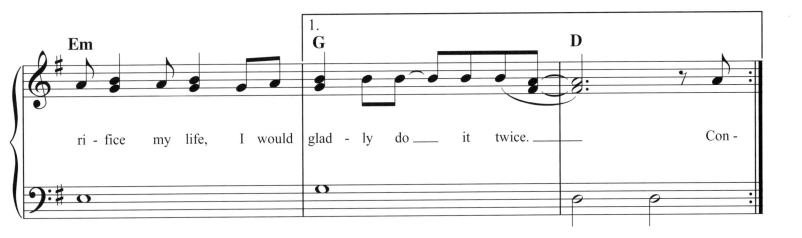

ri - fice my life, I would glad - ly do ____ it twice. ____ Con -

glad - ly do ____ it twice. ____ Oh, please have

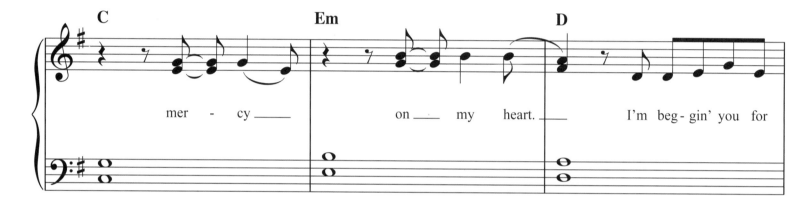

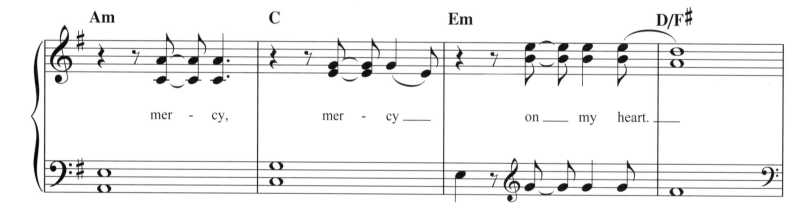

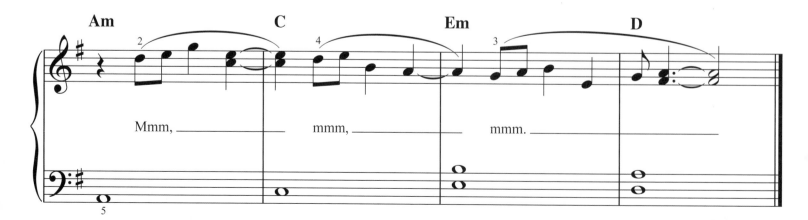

NEVER BE ALONE

Words and Music by SHAWN MENDES,
MARTIN TEREFE, GLEN SCOTT
and SCOTT FRIEDMAN

Moderate Folk

prom-ise that one day I'll be a - round. ___ I'll keep you safe, ___ I'll keep you sound.

Right now, it's pret-ty cra - zy and I don't know how to stop ___ or slow it down. ___

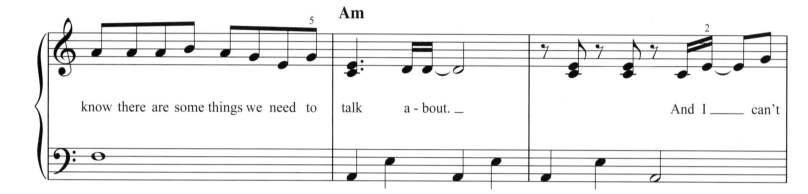

know there are some things we need to talk a-bout. And I can't

stay. Just let me hold you for a lit-tle long-er now.

Take a piece of my heart and make it all your

own   so when we are a - part   you'll nev-er be ___ a - lone. ___

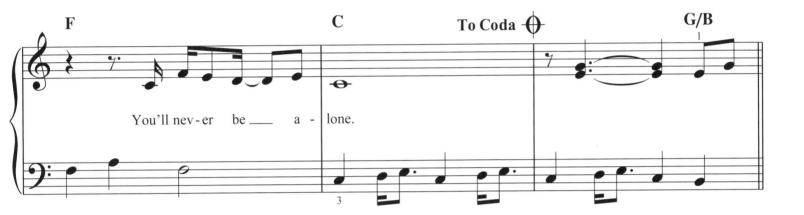

You'll nev - er   be ___ a - lone.

You'll nev - er be ___ a - lone. When you miss me close your

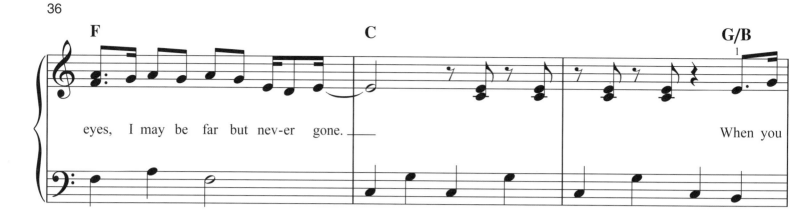

eyes, I may be far but nev-er gone. _____ When you

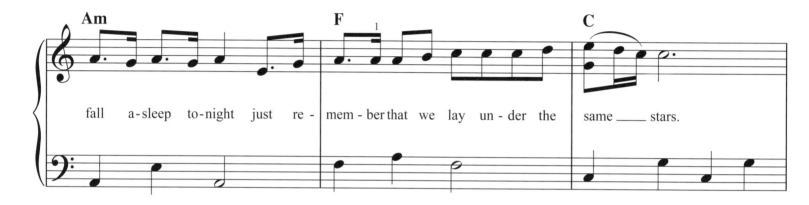

fall a-sleep to-night just re - mem-ber that we lay un-der the same _____ stars.

D.S. al Coda

CODA

You'll nev-er be ___ a - lone. ___ Oh, ___

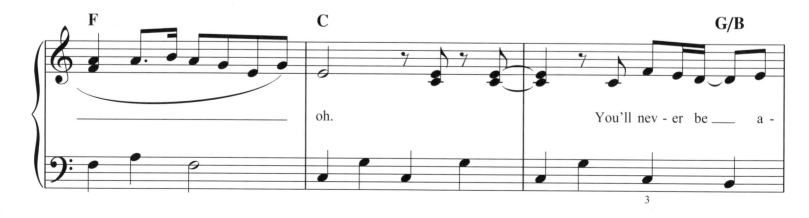

_____ oh.

You'll nev - er be ___ a -

3

lone. _____ Oh, _____ oh.

1. You'll nev - er be ___ a

2. And take a piece of my heart _

_____ and make it all your own so when we are a - part you'll nev - er be a -

lone. _____ You'll nev - er be a - lone. _____

MONSTER

Words and Music by JUSTIN BIEBER,
SHAWN MENDES, MUSTAFA AHMED,
ADAM FEENEY and ASHTON SIMMONDS

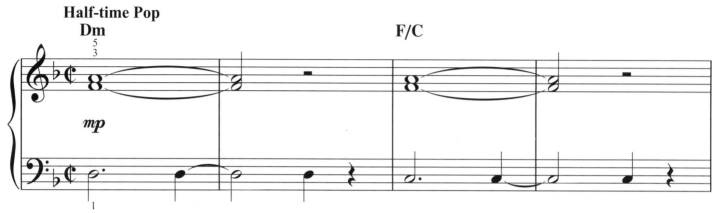

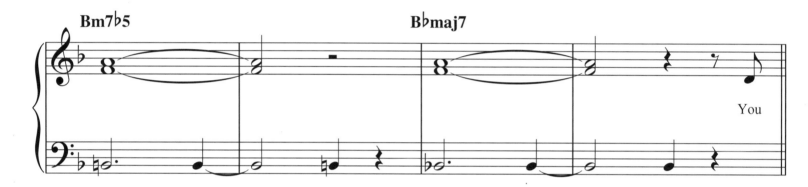

Dm

Fill me up with con - fi - dence, I say what's in my chest. __

C

Spill my words and tear me down un-

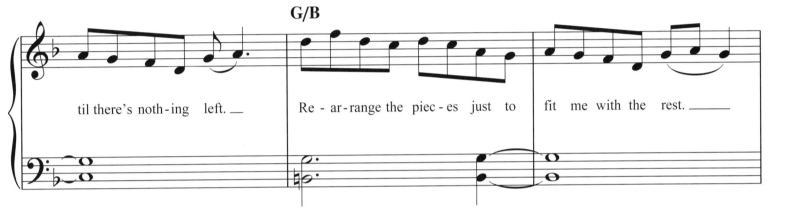

til there's noth - ing left. __

G/B

Re - ar - range the piec - es just to fit me with the rest. _____

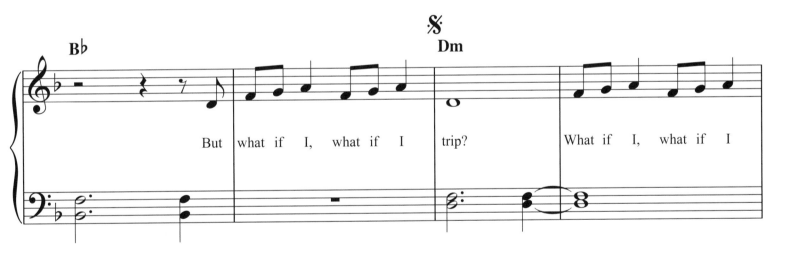

Bb

But what if I, what if I trip?

Dm

What if I, what if I

C

fall?

Then am I the mon - ster?

Gm

B♭ ... **Dm**

Just let me know._____ What if I, what if I sin?

C ... **Gm**

What if I, what if I break? Then am I the mon - ster?

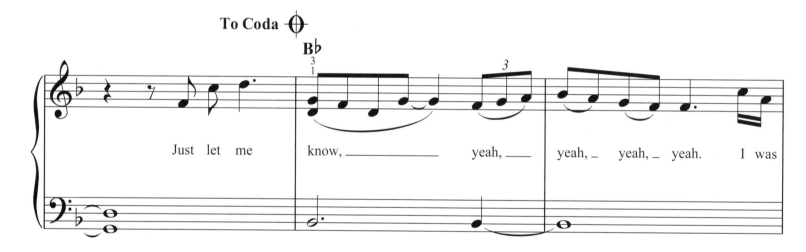

To Coda ⊕

B♭

Just let me know,_____ yeah,____ yeah,_ yeah,_ yeah. I was

N.C.

fif - teen when the world put me on a ped - es - tal. I had big dreams of do - ing shows_ and

mak-ing mem-o-ries. Made some bad moves, tryin' to act cool, up - set by their jeal-ous-y.

Dm

Lift-ing me up, lift-ing me up, and tear-ing me down,

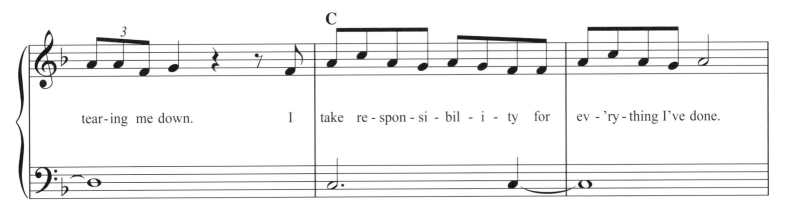

C

tear-ing me down. I take re-spon-si-bil-i-ty for ev-'ry-thing I've done.

Bm7♭5

B♭

Hold-ing it a-gainst me like you're the ho-ly one.

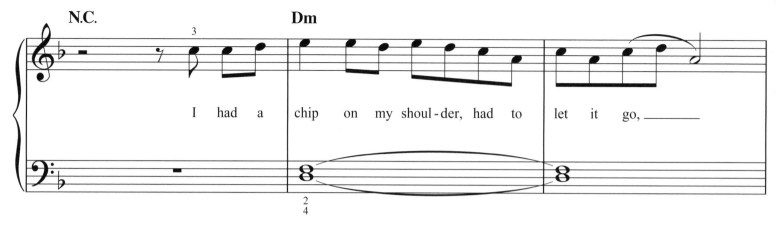

I had a chip on my shoul-der, had to let it go, _____

'cause un-for-give-ness keeps them in con-trol. _____ I came in with good in-ten-tions, then I

let it go. _____ And now I real-ly want to know. What if I

CODA

know. _____ (Oh, please, _____ just let me know.)

La da da da da da.

La da da da da da da na.

La da da da da da.

La da da da da da da na.

SEÑORITA

Words and Music by CAMILA CABELLO,
CHARLOTTE AITCHISON, JACK PATTERSON,
SHAWN MENDES, MAGNUS HOIBERG,
BENJAMIN LEVIN, ALI TAMPOSI
and ANDREW WOTMAN

Moderate Latin groove

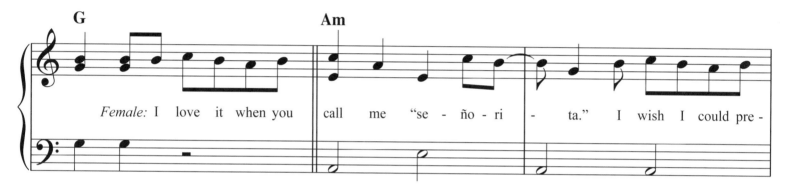

Female: I love it when you call me "se-ño-ri-ta." I wish I could pre-

tend I did-n't need ___ ya, but ev-'ry touch is ooh, la, ___ la, la. It's

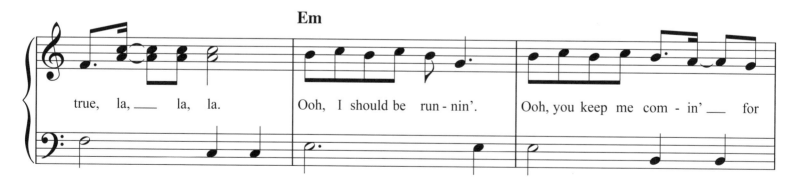

true, la, ___ la, la. Ooh, I should be run-nin'. Ooh, you keep me com-in' ___ for

Male:
ya. Land in Mi - am - i, the air was hot from sum-mer rain. Sweat drip-pin' off me.

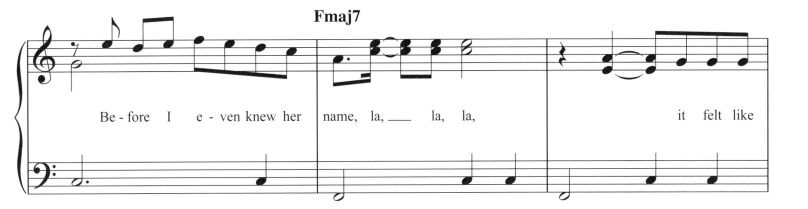

Be - fore I e - ven knew her name, la, ___ la, la, it felt like

ooh, la, ___ la, la. Yeah, ___ no. ___ Sap - phire ___ moon - light,

we danced for hours ___ in the sand. Te - qui - la sun - rise, her bod - y fit right in my

Fmaj7   **Em7**

hands, la, ____ la, la.   It felt like ooh, la, ____ la, la,   yeah. ____

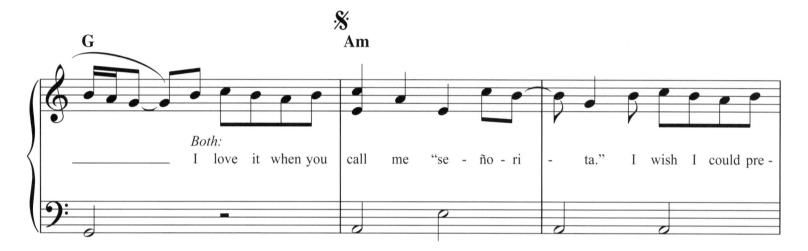

G   **Am**

Both:

_____ I love it when you call me "se-ño-ri-ta." I wish I could pre-

C   **F**

tend I did-n't need ____ ya, but ev-'ry touch is ooh, la, ____ la, la.   It's

                                      Em

true, la, ____ la, la.   Ooh, I should be run-nin'.   Ooh, you know I love it when you

call me "se - ño - ri - ta." I wish it was-n't so ____ hard to leave ____

____ ya, but ev - 'ry touch is ooh, la, ____ la, la. It's true, la, ____ la, la.

To Coda ⊕

Ooh, I should be run - nin'. Ooh, you keep me com - in' ____ for ya. Locked in the ho - tel,

Female:

there's just some things that nev - er change. You say we're just friends,

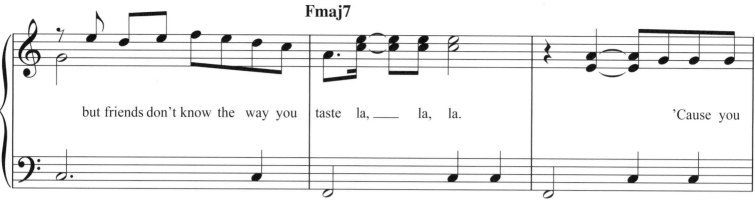

but friends don't know the way you taste la,____ la, la.   'Cause you

know it's been a long time com-in' don't you let me   fall,   oh._____

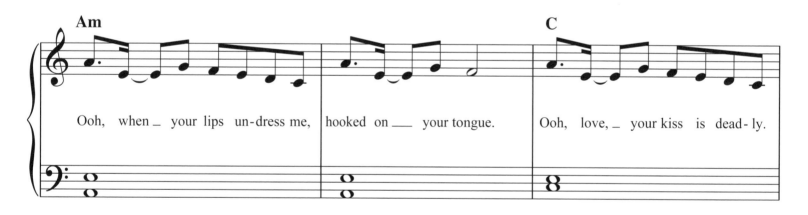

Ooh, when_ your lips un-dress me,   hooked on ___ your tongue.   Ooh, love,_ your kiss is dead-ly.

Both:
Don't stop. I love it when you

ya.   All a - long I'll___ be com-in'___ for

C   **Fmaj7**

ya.   And I hope it ___ meant some - thin' ___ to   ya.   Call my

Em7   **G**   **Am**

name I'll ___ be com - in' ___ for   ya.

C   **F**

Em7   **N.C.**

Ooh, I should be run - nin'.   Ooh, you keep me com - in' ___ for   ya.

SOMETHING BIG

Words and Music by SHAWN MENDES,
IDO ZMISHLANY and SCOTT FRIEDMAN

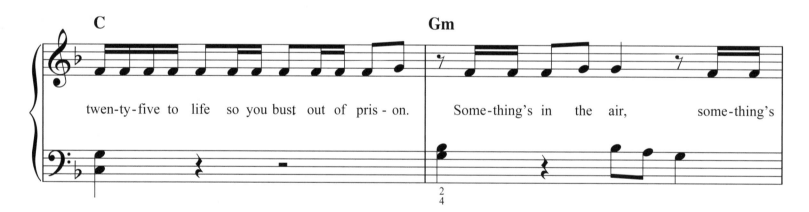

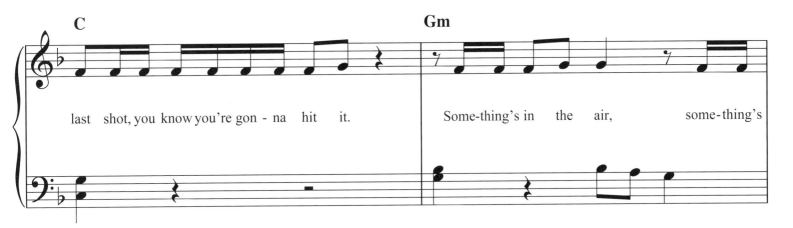

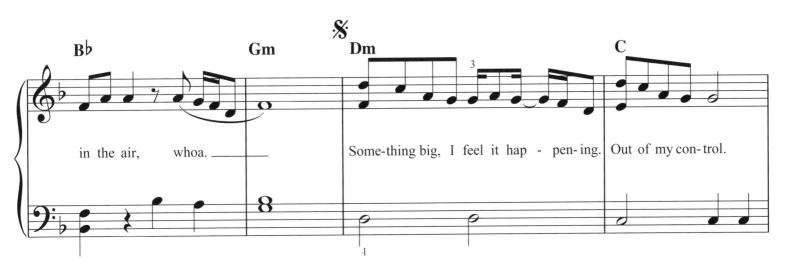

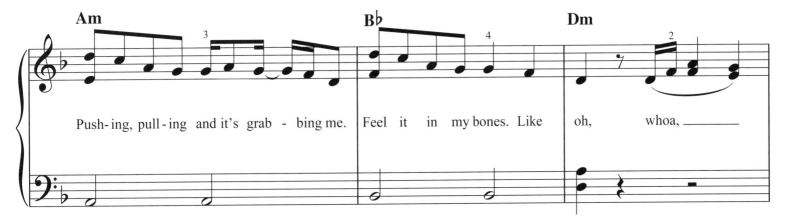

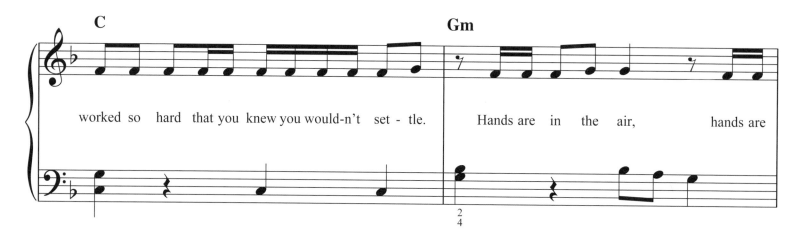

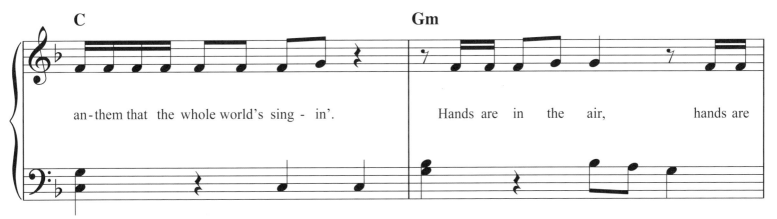

an-them that the whole world's sing - in'.　　Hands are in the air,　　hands are

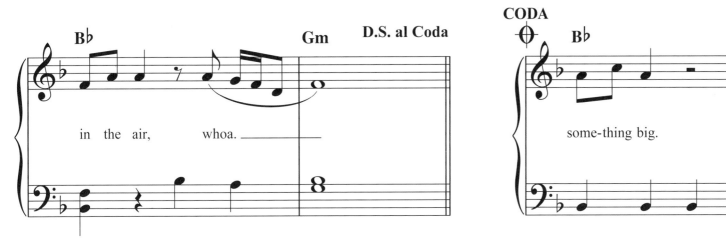

in the air,　whoa. ___　　　some-thing big.

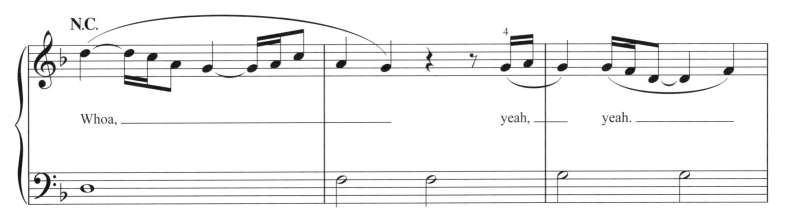

Whoa, ___　　　yeah, ___　yeah.

If we stomp our feet the ground _ will shake. _ If we

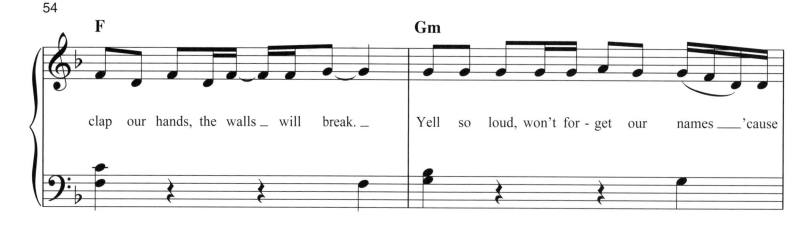

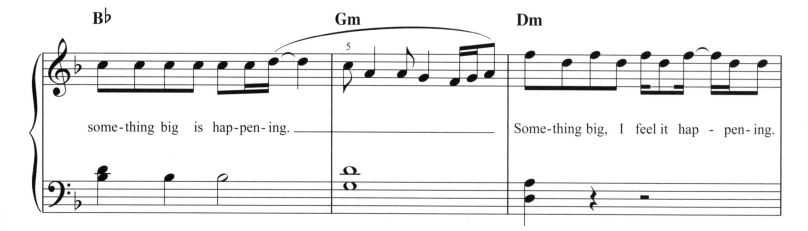

STITCHES

Words and Music by TEDDY GEIGER,
DANNY PARKER and DANIEL KYRIAKIDES

Moderate Latin groove

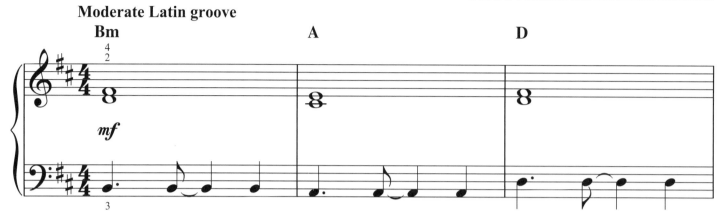

I thought that I'd been hurt be-fore

but no one's ev - er

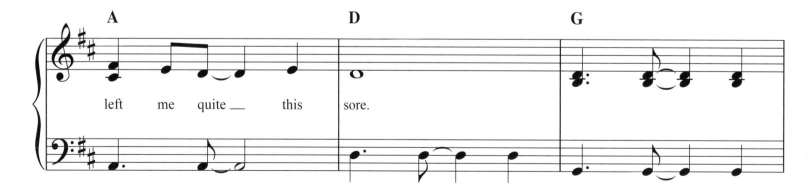

left me quite __ this sore.

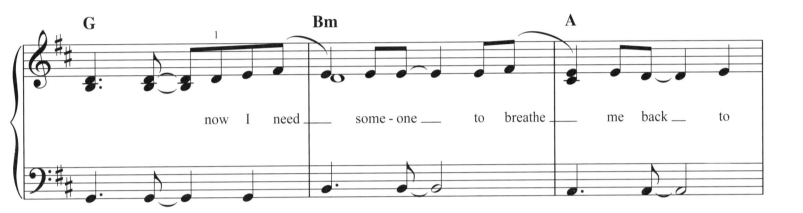

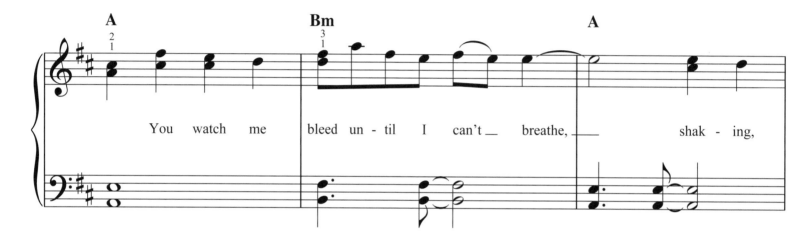

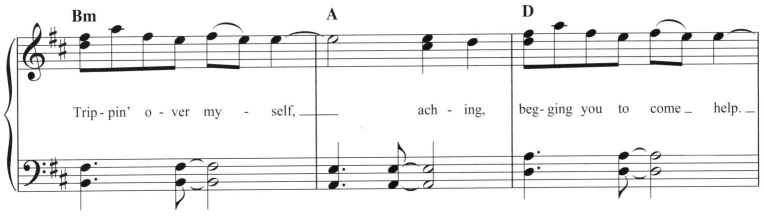

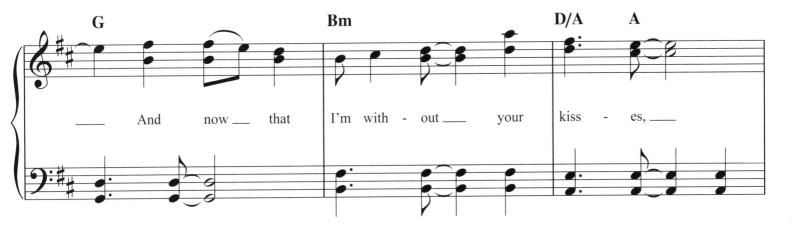

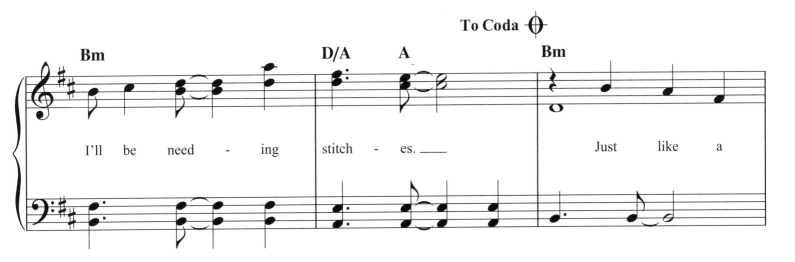

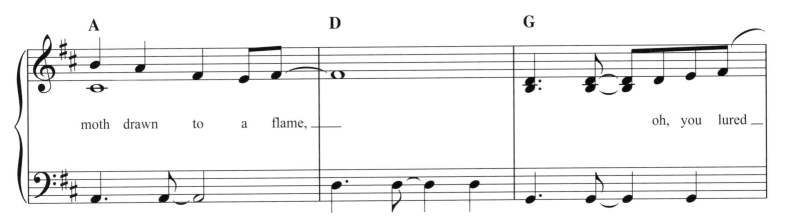

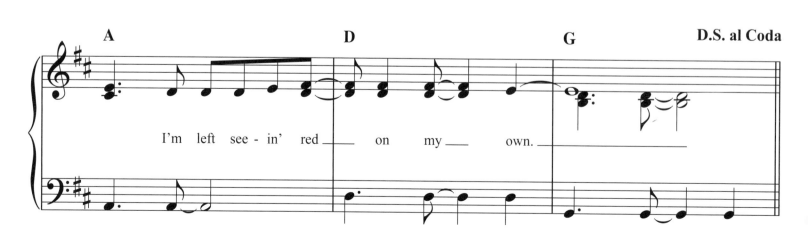

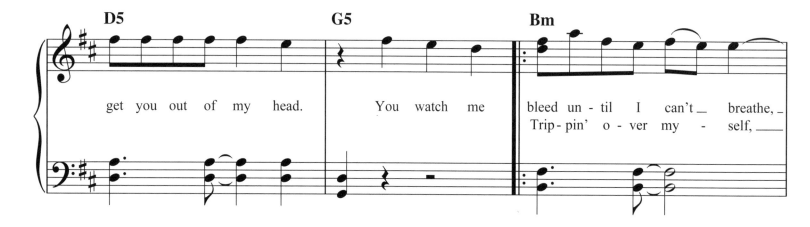

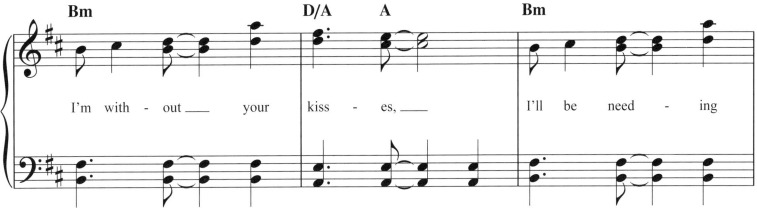

I'm with - out ___ your kiss - es, ___ I'll be need - ing

1. stitch - es. ___

2. stitch - es. Now ___ that I'm with - out ___ your

kiss - es, ___ I'll be need - ing stitch - es. Now ___ that

I'm with - out ___ your kiss - es, ___ I'll be need - ing stitch - es. ___

TREAT YOU BETTER

Words and Music by SHAWN MENDES,
SCOTT HARRIS and TEDDY GEIGER

Moderately, in 2

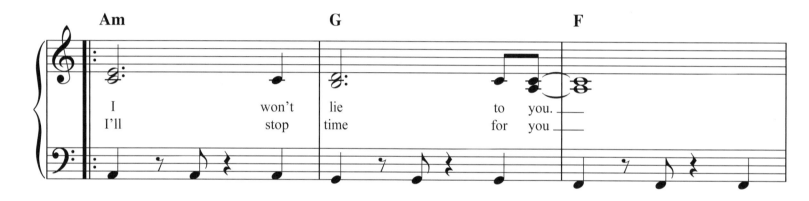

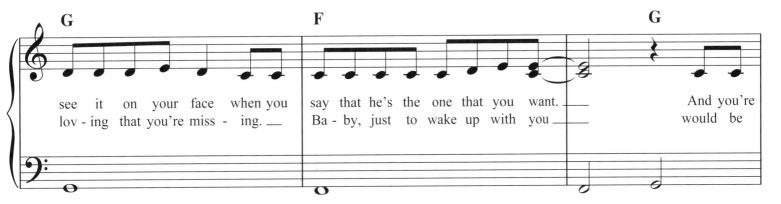

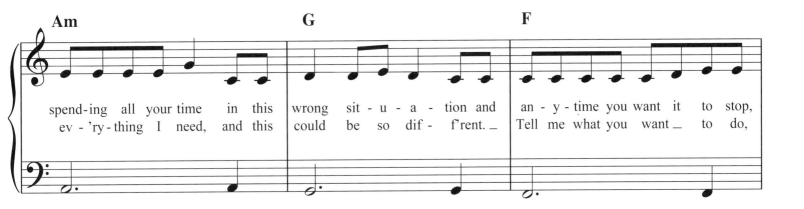

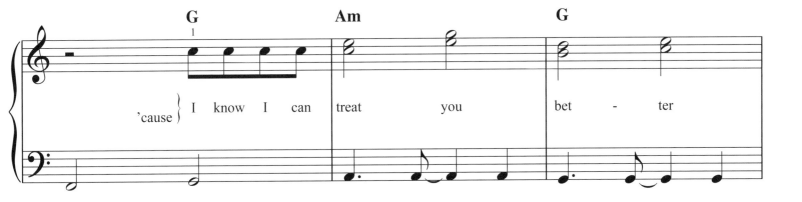

66

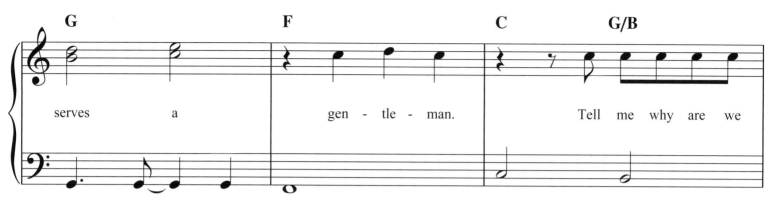

serves   a   gen - tle - man.   Tell me why are we

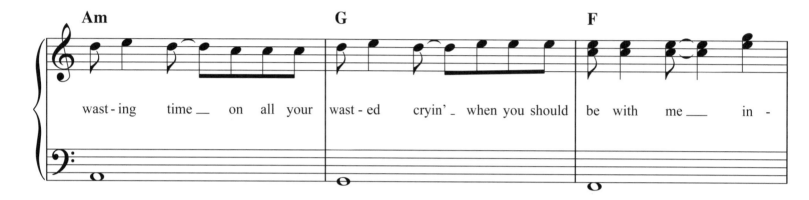

wast - ing   time ___ on all your   wast - ed   cryin' ___ when you should   be   with   me ___ in -

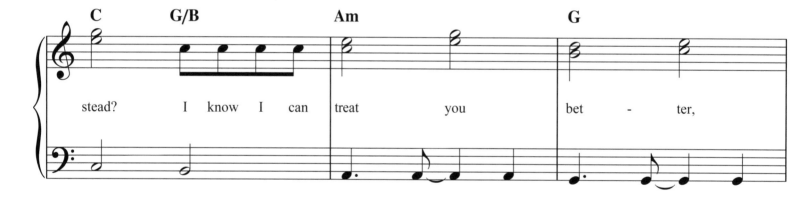

stead?   I know I can   treat   you   bet - ter,

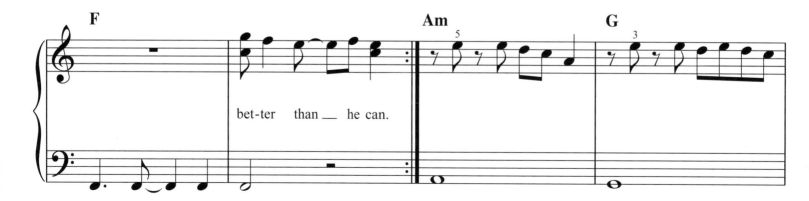

bet - ter   than ___ he can.

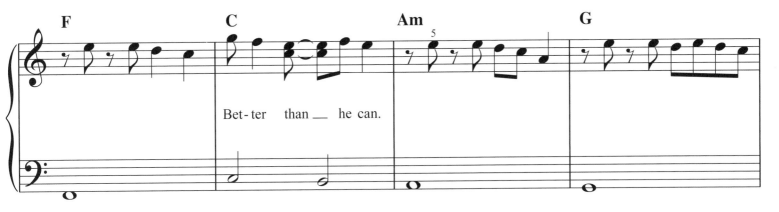

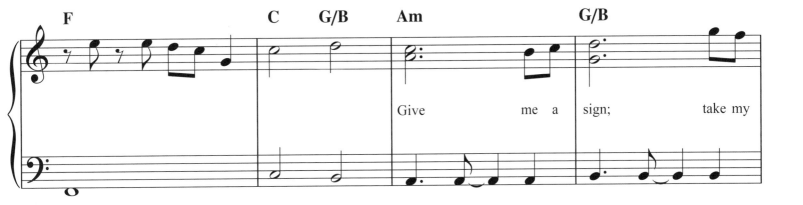

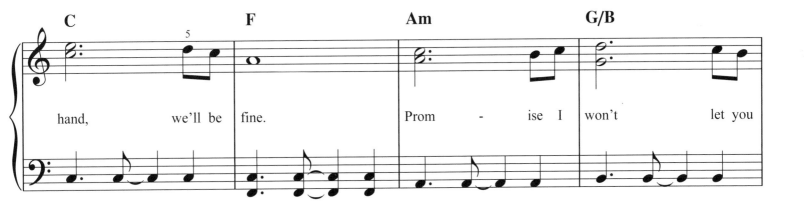

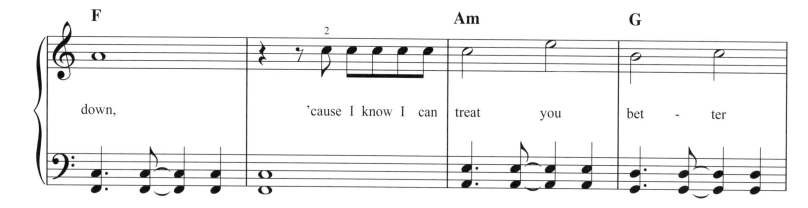

G   F   C   G/B

wast - ed   cryin' _ when you should   be with   me _   in - stead?   I know I can

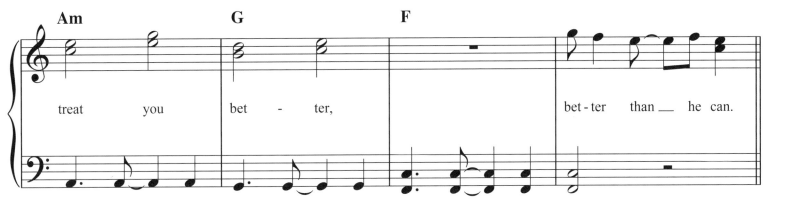

Am   G   F

treat   you   bet   -   ter,   bet - ter   than _ he can.

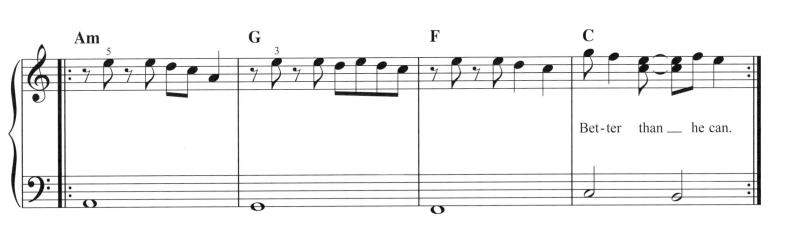

Am   G   F   C

Bet - ter   than _ he can.

Am   G   F   C   Am

WONDER

Words and Music by SHAWN MENDES,
THOMAS HULL, SCOTT HARRIS
and NATE MERCEREAU

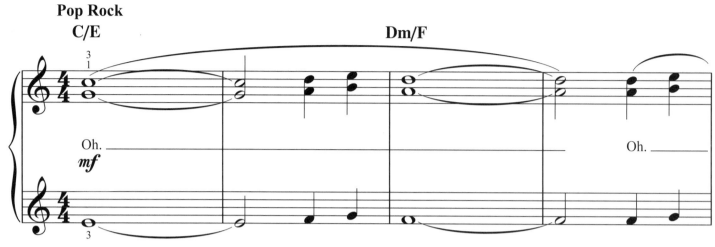

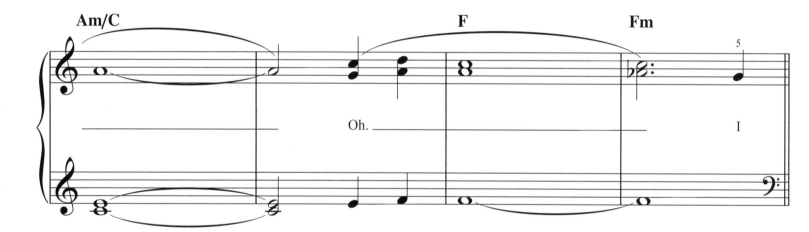

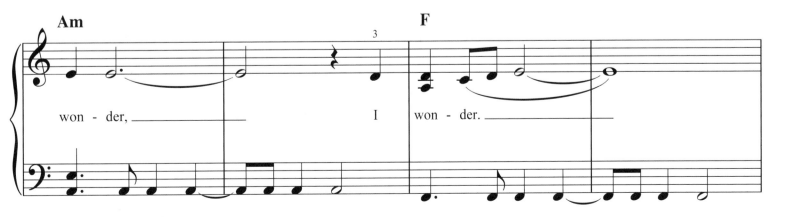

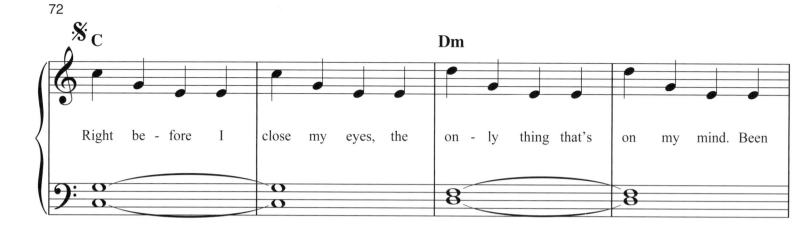

Right be - fore I | close my eyes, the | on - ly thing that's | on my mind. Been

dream - ing that you | feel it too, I | won - der what it's | like to be loved by

you. _____ | Yeah. _____ | I | won - der what it's like. _

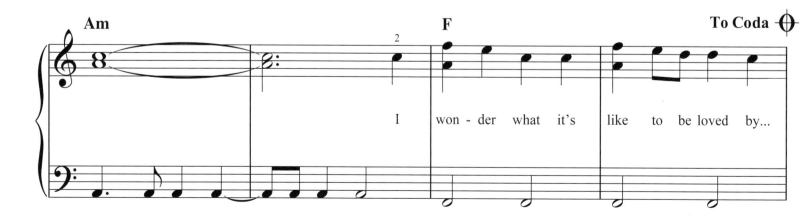

I | won - der what it's | like to be loved by...

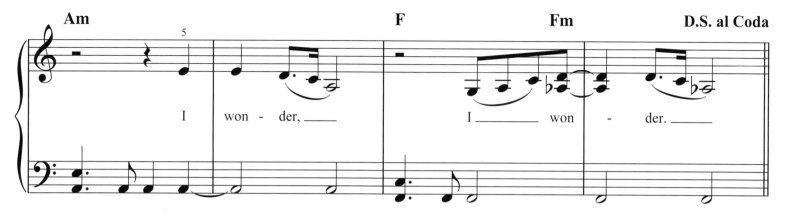

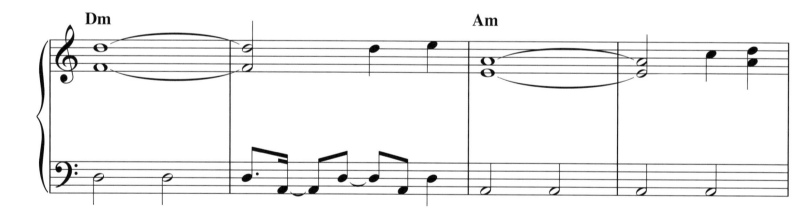

THERE'S NOTHING HOLDIN' ME BACK

Words and Music by SHAWN MENDES,
GEOFFREY WARBURTON, TEDDY GEIGER
and SCOTT HARRIS

Acoustic Pop

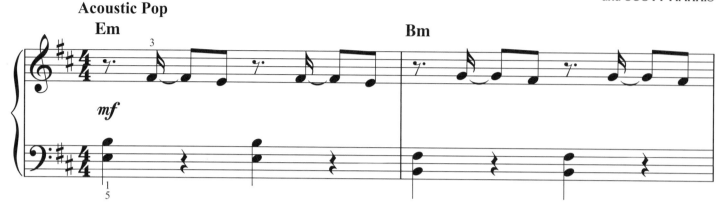

I want to fol-low where she goes,
She says that she's nev-er a-fraid;

I think a-bout her and she
just pic-ture ev-'ry-bod-y

knows it.
na-ked.

I want to let her take con-trol,
She real-ly does-n't like to wait,

'cause ev - 'ry time that she gets clos - er, she pulls
not real - ly in - to hes - i - ta - tion. Pulls me in e -

nough to keep ___ me guess - ing. ___ Mm. ___

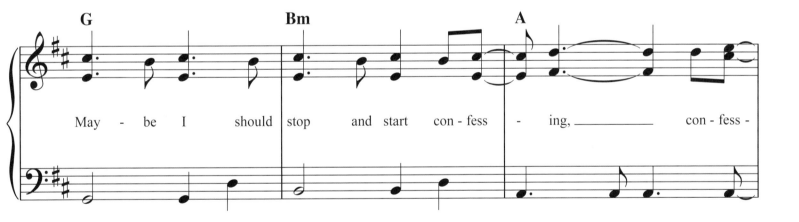

May - be I should stop and start con - fess - ing, ___ con - fess -

- ing, yeah. ___ Oh, I've been shak - ing, I love you when you go cra - zy. You take

all my in - hi - bi - tions, ba - by, there's noth-ing hold- in' me back. You take me plac - es that tear

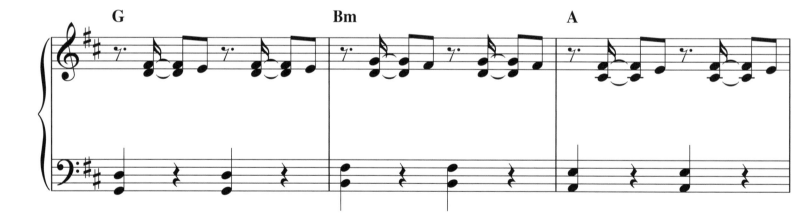

up my rep - u - ta - tion, ma - nip - u - late my de - ci - sions. Ba - by, there's noth-ing hold- in' me back.

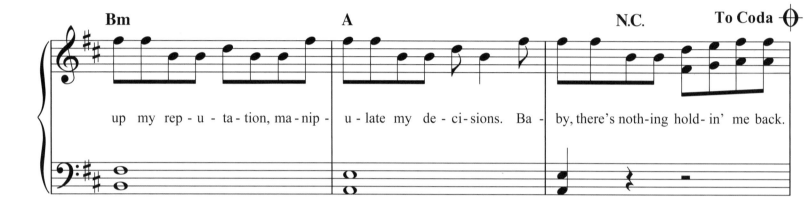

There's noth-ing hold- in' me back.

There's noth-ing hold-in' me back. 'Cause if we

lost our minds and we took it way too far, I know we'd be al-right, I know we would be al-right. If you were

by my side and we stum-bled in the dark, I know we'd

be al-right, I know we would be al-right, 'Cause if we lost our minds and we took

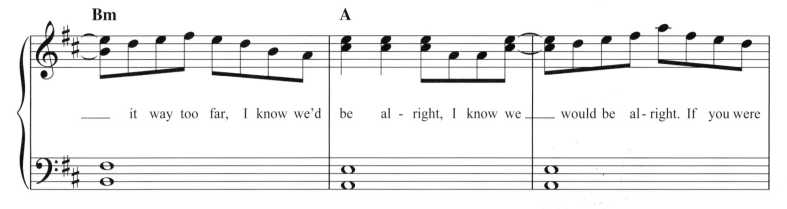

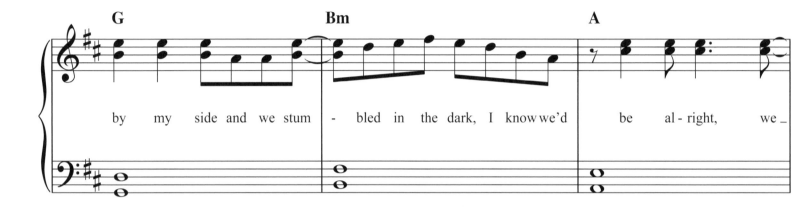

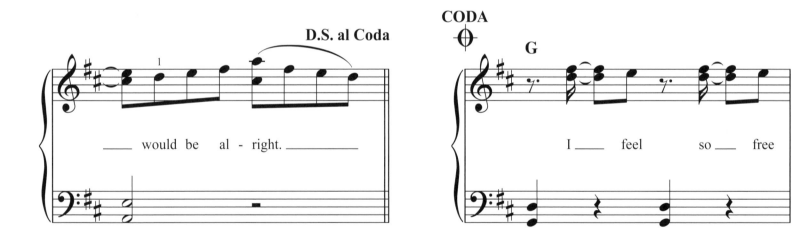